My First Sticker by NUMBERS Book

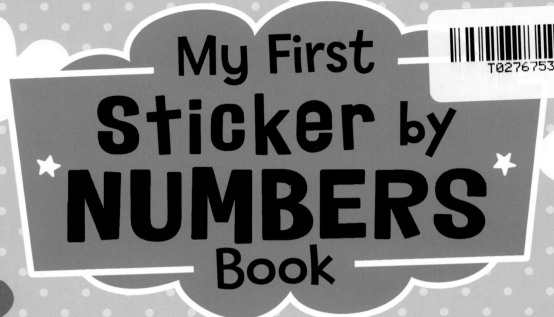

Illustrated by **Alice Griffiths**

PSS!
PRICE STERN SLOAN
An Imprint of Penguin Random House

T0276753

How to Use This Book

Create amazing pictures using the colored stickers at the back of this book.

The pictures in this book contain numbered white shapes. Your job is to cover these white areas with stickers that are the correct color and shape by following the number code. The numbers on the shapes are also colored to help you.

5

Concept and editorial by Lauren Farnsworth
Design by Jack Clucas, Cover Design by Angie Allison

PRICE STERN SLOAN
Penguin Young Readers Group
An Imprint of Penguin Random House LLC

ISBN 9780451532367

1 Look at the colored number on each white shape—this matches the number on the same colored sheet of stickers at the back of the book.

2 Choose the correct-shape sticker from the sticker page. You can pull out the sticker pages so they are easier to use.

3 Stick this sticker over the white shape on the page. Fill in all the white shapes to create brilliant pictures.

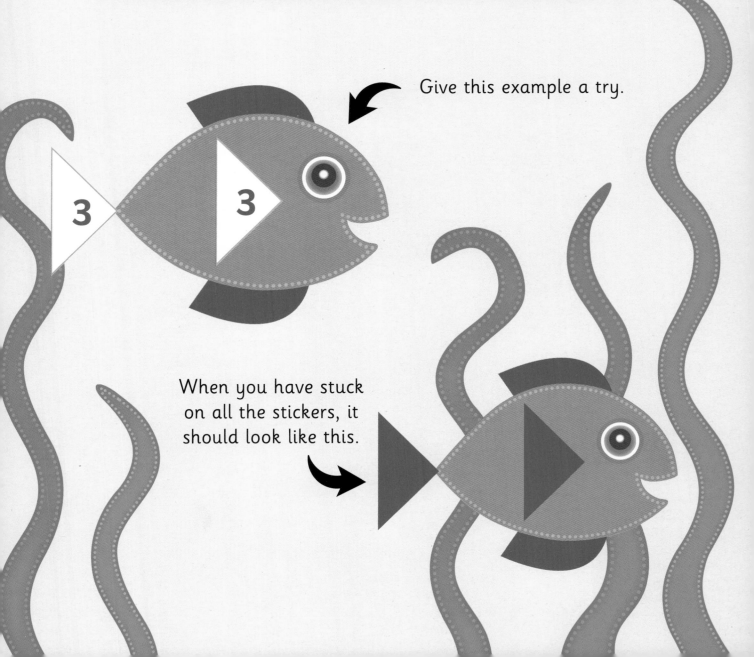

Give this example a try.

When you have stuck on all the stickers, it should look like this.

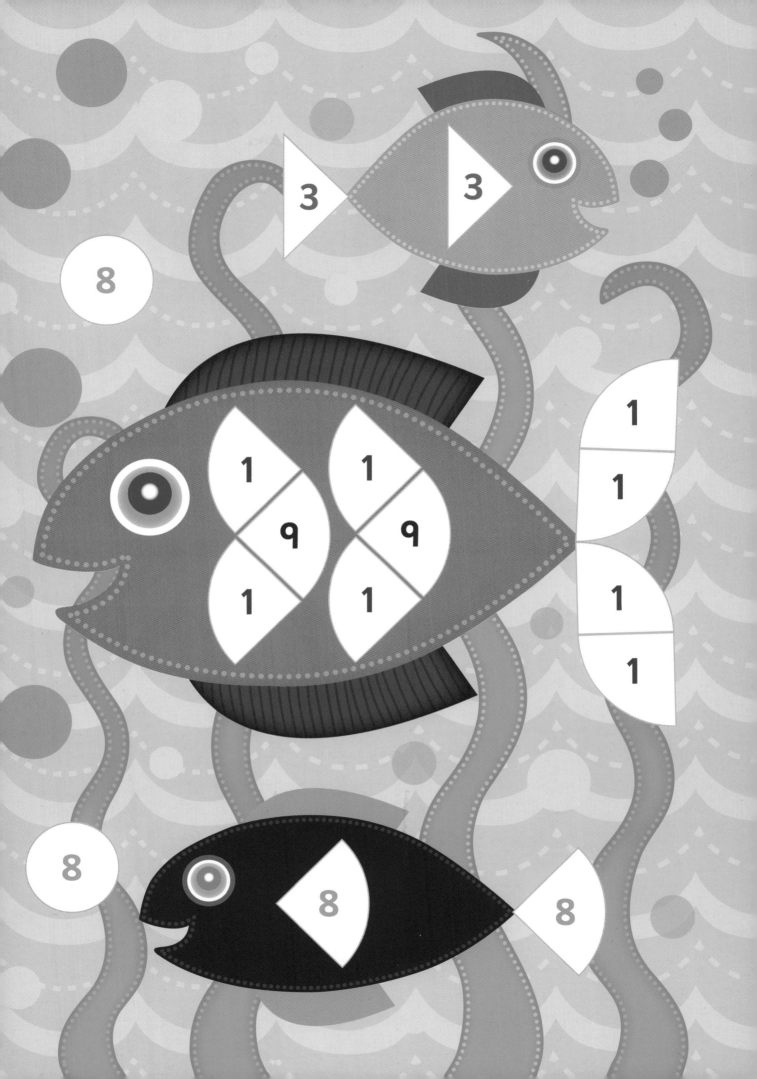

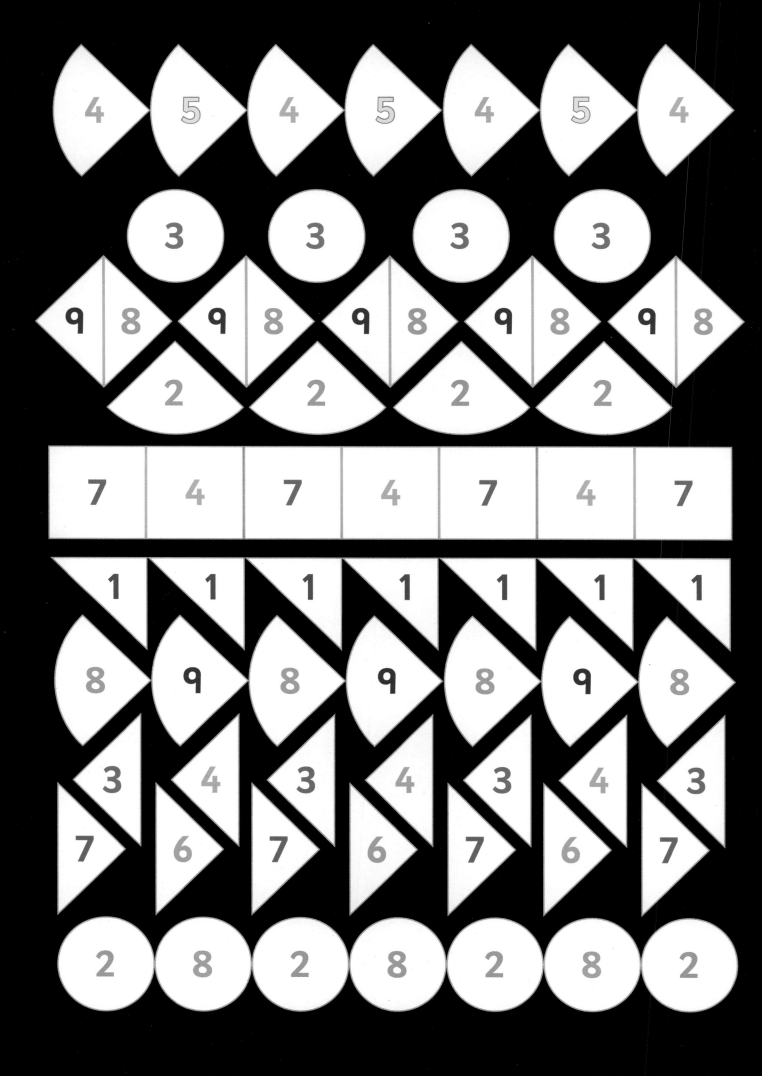

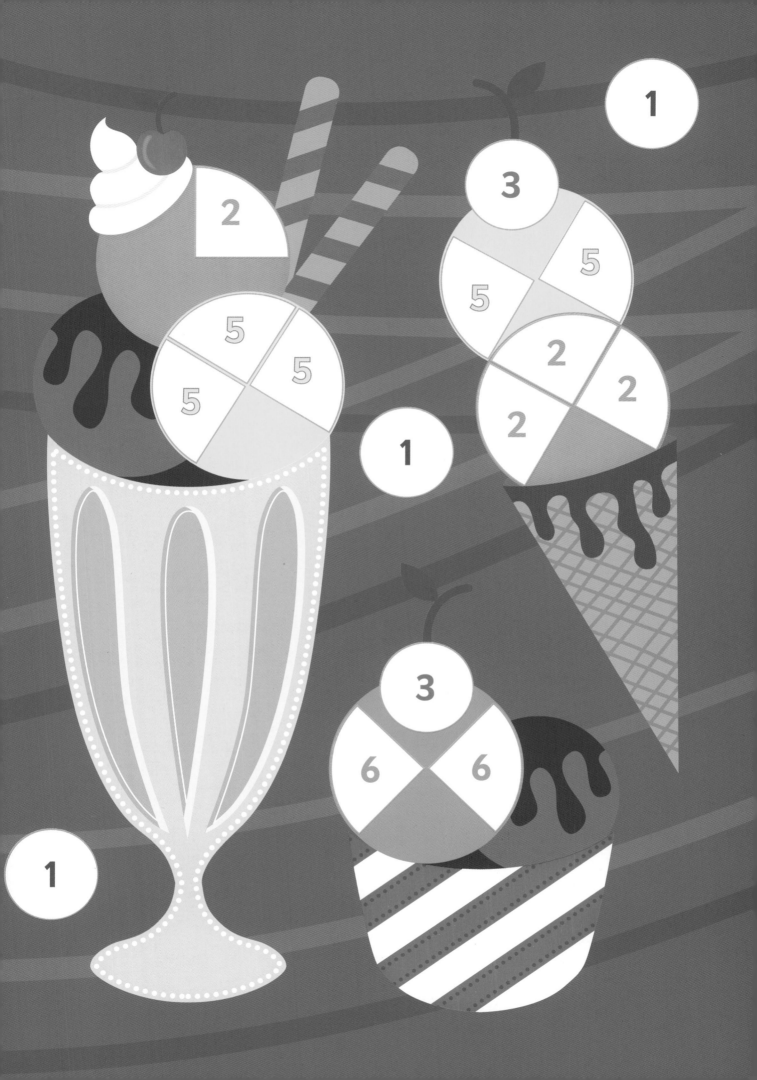

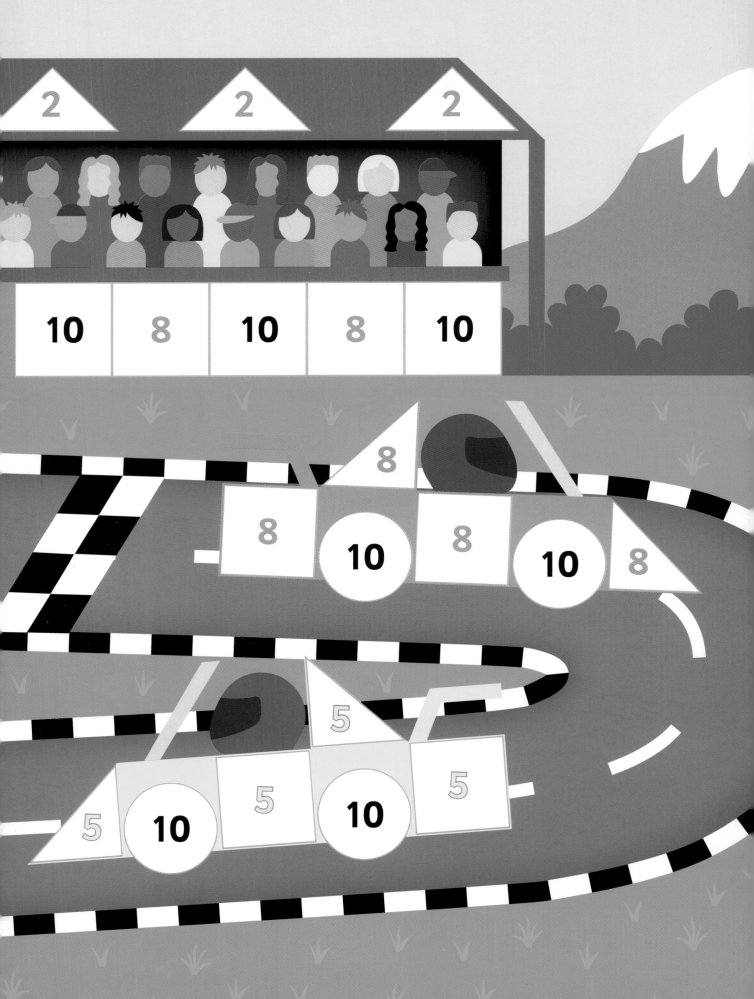

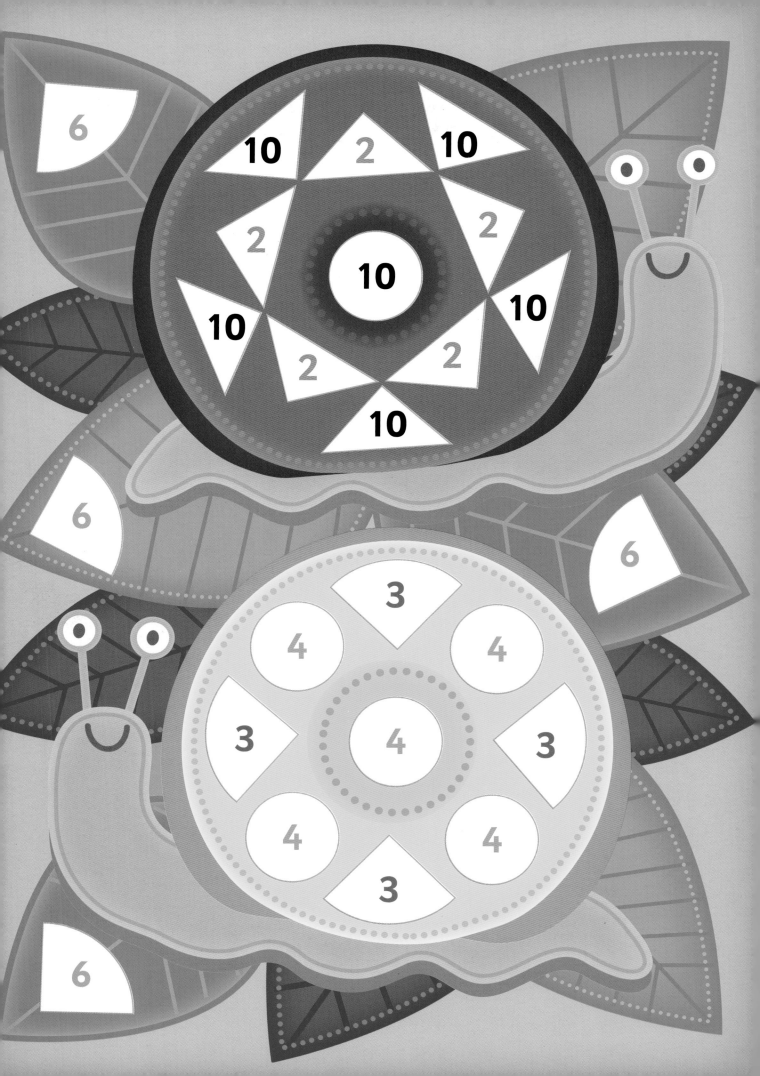

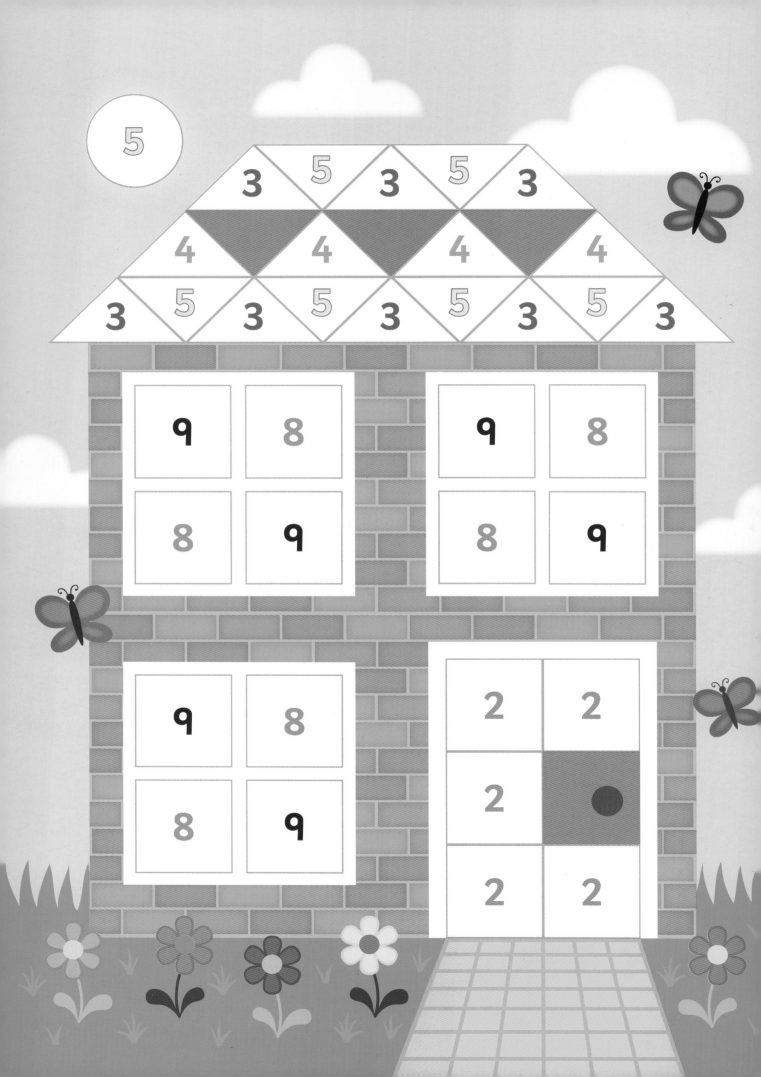